T0077640

# Art, Tribes, & Cultures
## Identify Us

# Art, Tribes, & Cultures Identify Us

## DAMOLA TAIWO

iUniverse, Inc.
Bloomington

## Art, Tribes, & Cultures Identify Us

Copyright © 2008, 2011 by Damola Taiwo.

All rights reserved. No part of this book may be used or reproduced by any means, graphic, electronic, or mechanical, including photocopying, recording, taping or by any information storage retrieval system without the written permission of the publisher except in the case of brief quotations embodied in critical articles and reviews.

Dst African collages
Registration number: va 1-014-835

Dst African paintings serires 2& 3
Registration number: vau 475-510
Effective date:Dec 2, 1999

Damo tribe dvd: dvd comes with book
But not enclosed to the book yet
Registration number: pau 3-540-830
Effective date: march 17,2008

Dst African paintings "8"
Registration number: vau 527-659
Effective date: July 05, 2001

Copyright claimant: Damola Taiwo

( David) nick name

iUniverse books may be ordered through booksellers or by contacting:

iUniverse
1663 Liberty Drive
Bloomington, IN 47403
www.iuniverse.com
1-800-Authors (1-800-288-4677)

Because of the dynamic nature of the Internet, any web addresses or links contained in this book may have changed since publication and may no longer be valid. The views expressed in this work are solely those of the author and do not necessarily reflect the views of the publisher, and the publisher hereby disclaims any responsibility for them.

Any people depicted in stock imagery provided by Thinkstock are models, and such images are being used for illustrative purposes only.
Certain stock imagery © Thinkstock.

ISBN: 978-1-4620-4336-1 (sc)
ISBN: 978-1-4620-4337-8 (ebk)

Printed in the United States of America

iUniverse rev. date: 08/15//2012

# Contents

**DAMOLA TAIWO**
MOVIE PICTURES 2006

*Tribal logo*

*created by*

*Damola Taiwo*

©2008 ALL Rights reserved Damola t.

# Definition

The word "**Art**" means a lot to all of us (human). According to my definition, our creativities and crafts come in form of art. Since, I grew up in Africa. I can illustrate my point. My source of art was taken from West Africa (experience). Therefore, I believe I can express myself in the geographical work of African art.

**Art** shapes define the world. These definitions are the maps, furniture, pools, cars, stoves, electronics, houses, mountains, clothes, squares, triangles, spheres, cylinders, pyramids, prism, cones, and the human body. Therefore, we survive through the means of art.

The **Art**, **Tribe,** and **Culture** identifies our heritages. These three categories identify our ways of qualities in life. These qualities identify us (human). These three categories allow us to survive in this universe. As a main source of income on surviving, we can use our artistic endeavors. These artistic endeavors indicate our activities, lives, and occupations. This means "**God**" has given and blessed us **(human)** on what we need to survive in this universe. In this universe, we (Human) have the strength and power within us to survive. This means **whatever** and **wherever** you originated from, art represents you. However, you do not have to be perfect. In this universe, the art within you will be observed by the people. Singing, drawing, engineering, computer gaming, and other means of art. It could be the hidden art within you. And you have the capabilities of achieving your arististic endeavors.

# Colors Of Africa

# COLORS OF AFRICA

# COLORS OF AFRICA

MOTHERLAND-AFRICA: OIL ON CANVAS

HAPPINESS-AFRICA: ACRYLIC ON CANVAS

## COLORS OF AFRICA
### THE AFRICAN KING

**BEAUTIFUL GIRL**

# COLORS OF AFRICA

DEPRESSION:OIL/CANVAS

THE CRY:OIL ON CANVAS

# COLORS OF AFRICA

IN LOVE:MIXED MEDIA ON PAPER

FREE WORLD:MIXED MEDIA ON PAPER

# COLORS OF AFRICA

NO RESPECT: OIL ON WOOD

THE CARELESS MOTHER: OIL ON CANVAS

The Africans have three main colors they use in their drawings. These colors are red, blue, and gold. Each color symbolizes what they went through in life. For example, gold symbolizes success, which means the Africans have conquered or defeated suffering. For example, when the Africans are happy, they wear bright color outfits such as yellow, gold, blue, and peach.

Africa is defined as modes of colors in form **of art**. These **colors** consist of the African kingdom and facial expressions of the people. However, African countries are successful in the work of Arts. In Africa, there are great forests and abundant natural wealth.

**In Africa**, the artists express their feelings in colors through form of painting. And these **colors** can be observed.

Africa is well known for its rich artistic endeavor. This artistic endeavor can be observed from the African outfits. These fabrics are called aso oke, adire, and the fi la (the hat). These fabrics are not very common in foreign countries. In African countries, these fabrics are very common. Because they were produced there by the artists and the fashion designers. These fabrics are traditional outfits for the Africans. These fabrics are 100 percent cotton and they last a life time.

*Reference / Info:*
*Check listing: Art: The forest:* Damola Art Studio / Damola Interactive / Damola Technology / Chicago

# Symbol Of My Art

I always use gold color in my painting to symbolize success. I always use gold color when I conquer negativity in my life. I used "animation" to interpret my paintings. And that symbolizes my strength in the work of art. I used yellow, cool blues, bright greens, and oranges. This symbolizes success and victory in my painting. In West Africa, my drawing and painting expresses my life experience. The symbol of my art shows the celebration of my tribe and culture. The Yoruba tribe is the symbol of my art works. The symbolic expressions found on my characters indicate my artwork. The hand gestures and body languages interpret my work. The movement of my brush strokes interpret my art works. In my paintings, my brush strokes are animated and symbolic. My logo icon {tribe} represents my work and who I am.

# Geographical Color
# Of Africa

# GEOGRAPHICAL COLORS OF AFRICA
## THE AFRICAN FOREST:LOVERS:MIXED MEDIA

THE AFRICAN VILLAGE:MIXED MEDIA/PAPER

These art forms of color shows safari, forest, **high mountains**, **falls,** and **wild life** species. The African artists draw from what they see in the geographical part of Africa. From our observation, African artists show the safari with dry soil and less Water (paintings). Certainly, we can believe we draw from our live experiences. From our observation, art is created with different approaches and different feelings.

In the **African forest**, African artists draw from what they see visually. This art consists of beautiful colorful birds. The colors of the African birds used are red, yellow, green, orange, and blue. From African art, we see the flow movement of flying colorful birds and water. From my art, animation can be observed through the form of water. Creatively, the water flows from the left and right directions.

Let us discuss about the geographical section of the **African forest**. We know snakes are present in the forest. We know some of the snakes in the deep forests are wild. However, some parts have amusement zoos for the wild species (parks). Therefore, we believe the artist would draw roughly to indicate the endangered species of African art.

# Wild Species Of Africa

# WILD SPECIES OF AFRICA

ROUGH SKETCH

# WILD SPECIES OF AFRICA

According to the wild species, there are lions, tigers, cheetahs, Rhinos, zebras, chimpanzees, and others. These **wild species** move freely in an open air space region. These animals move freely around, so you are not required to **pay** to see them. However, **caution** should be required, while around these **wild animals**. The elephants, zebras, donkeys are friendly animals. The chimpanzees, lions, tigers, cheetahs, & rhinos are considered to be wild species. However, the cheetah is well known as the fastest animal on land. The cheetah has quite an impressive speed ratio.

# Two Regions Of Africa

In Africa, each country has two regions. The African region is divided into two parts. These regions are the city environment and the suburban environment. The city environment is the advanced section of Africa. In the city environment, there are tall commercial buildings and residential buildings. In the city part of Africa, we have development of business, banking, and self trades. Some of the people are self employed in the city and suburban area of Africa. In the city part of Africa, there are wealthy amenities. In the deep suburban region of Africa, there are great shrines, roads, rivers, deep forests, mountains, safaris, villages, and renovated houses. In the suburban region of Africa, there are hunters, farmers, and the poultry industries. In the poultry industry, we have the chickens and egg factory. The great farmers bring the completed enriched foods into the city for trading. From my artistic observation, The tools used for farming were created and designed in the work of art.

The African suburb consists of tall and short trees. In the suburbs, there are **trees** filled with all kinds of fruits. These fruits are coconuts, mangoes, bananas, pawpaw, pineapples, cocoa, guava, oranges, red plantains, & coffee nuts. The wilderness and safari consists of wild animals (moving around). These wild animals are lions, tigers, cheetahs, Rhinos, Buffalo, and others.

# Occupations Of Africa

OCCUPATION OF AFRICANS

THE AFRICAN DRUMMER

The occupations of the Africans are weaving of braids, dyeing of fabrics, fine arts, trading of goods, construction of houses, gold mining, hunting, farming, and agriculture. In Africa, there are natural resources such as gas, oil, palm oil, coffee, coal, gold, diamond, and others. One of the natural resources can be used as petroleum for the automobiles.

However, some of the great workers can tend to change to self-employed workers. These great self employed workers are known as the community workers or community contractors. The contractors build houses and great roads for the community. This occupation is used as a great foundation to improve the landscape of Africa. The contractor employs the workers to build the houses and the roads. From the community, the contractor can generate income on the completed project. The first class jobs are the community workers and the self-employed workers. In the community, the self-employed workers can rent stores. These imported goods are shoes, cars, electronics, high quality jeans, and others. In the community, the self-employed can rent a store. These rented stores can be used to sell the imported goods to the people and public. The people have the privilege to benefit from the imported goods                                                    .

The first class and **middle class** workers consist of the bankers, art designers, art directors, movie producers, furniture designers, architects, computer graphic designers, programmers, and secretaries.

In the community, there are other great class jobs. These other great jobs are burger joint restaurant chefs, bus drivers, mechanics, housekeepers, and construction workers. However, other great class workers can tend to change to entrepreneurs.

### Dictionary: Business trade:

**Export**: selling abroad or sending natural resources to other foreign countries as business trade transactions to benefit its country. Examples: coffee, palm oil, petroleum & wood sculptures.

**Import**: bringing in or trading in other country resources to its country. Example, canned food: baked beans, peas, pears, cereals, baby foods, & apples. Imported clothes: polo shirts, wrist watches, jeans, and cologne, etc.

**Foreign exchange for industries:** exchanging natural resources & goods as business trade transactions. This business trade is processed by negotiating and bargaining between two countries.

Examples: cell phones, DVD players, lap tops, TVs, and computers.

# Origination Of African Art

# ORIGINATION OF MY WORK

*My sketches define my tribe*

*..my culture*

# ORIGINATION OF MY WORK

I do it my way, my tribe, my culture...
...sometimes, breaking little rules in art
doesn't hurt..!
the rubberlike drawing...
that's me.
peace,
Damola taiwo

**Weaving** and **braids** were originated from the African continent. That taste of weaving and braids identify the Africans. Weaving and braids are described as visual art. The word "visual" means what we can see with our **eyes**. This means **'braids'** can not be observed internally, but externally(visual).

The visual art shows us where we come from {**origination**) in the universe. For instance, We know every continent in the universe has its own work of art. From my artistic observation, there are great works of arts in Mexican art, American art, Asian art, Indian art, European art, African art, and others. This defines "us" as great and unique people in the world.

This visual creativity extends to other visual skills such as drawings, dyeing of fabrics, and sculpting. The Africans dye clothes in permanent ink coating liquid form of art. The application of color and style defines the origination of the art.

# Comparison To Other World Of Art

The origination of art predicts the work of a country. The origination of art predicts the style, flow and movement of the work. The origination of my culture predicts my artworks (paintings). In West Africa, I sketched what I have seen in my day to day life experience. These experiences were chasing the animals, climbing the trees, farming, playing with the lizards, soccer playing, and tribal dancing. My other best experiences were traveling, climbing mountains, cooking, and tasting of great dishes of the world. Creatively, learning and appreciating other people's cultures were my favorites. This creates comparison between my artistic endeavors and other great people of the world.

From my experience, I can define how I feel about other artist's art works (painting). I can compare my art to other countries in the world. The word "Imitation" is not my lifestyle. I draw what is on my mind and within my tribe. According to my artworks, I can say I draw in a **free form** process of art. I will disagree that I imitate other artist's work. And that separates my art work from other artists. In this universe, people learn to imitate other masters in art. A great example, I have read and seen other great masters in the historical works of arts at the museums. These great famous artists were Picasso, Vah Gogh, Michelangelo and others. From my artistic observation, they have highly impressive styles in drawings and paintings. They have the greatest artworks that I have ever seen in the world. Artistically, I admired the historical art works of Michelangelo. Michelangelo was very talented in his artistic works. Michelangelo completed some of his architectural and sculptural projects. I was reading about Michelangelo's work and I realized he continued in his last years to write poetry. Artistically, we all have different points of observation. From my own artistic and historical observation about art, I can assume

**"not all heads are the same"**.

One artist's skills will be better than other artists. Because we are not made the same way. I always have respect for the masters of art. **Michelangelo** has the greatest skills of all time.

# Cultures Of One
# African Country

CULTURE OF AFRICA

According to my observation about cultures, a language describes the origination of a culture. The culture can be recognized by the way we dress too (styles). The fabric can be used to describe the type of culture within the environment. Culturally, everyone does not dress the same way (background). Every culture has its own great way of dressing. The African females wear **braids** and head ties on their heads. The African braids come in various forms of art patterns. These braids are micro—braids and corn—braids. The cultural aspect of Africa can also be observed in salutations. In a respectful way, Africans greet each other (Africans). In respect of the Yoruba community, the **females** kneel down and greet their elders. And the **males** bend down flat on the floor and greet the elders.And sometimes, lay flat on the floor. The salutation is used with "**sir**" or "**ma**".

The Yoruba community greets this way to show respect for their elders.

# Art Of Speech To Other Countries

For example, a foreigner visits Africa. The foreigner can be observed.
As a state of the foreigner's accent (**art of speech / pitch tone**).The African could assume the visitor is a foreigner (**location / pitch tone**). However, the Africans would not know what part of America. America has good reputation of great large cities within its continent and beautiful places. Certainly, every other continent in the world consists of beautiful places and great cultural aspects. Creatively and naturally, we are all blessed. We all have creative skills within us. Europe, Africa, Asia, America are continents. Within these continents, we have numerous countries.

From my observation about African arts, interesting artworks can be observed. Artworks can be observed in different great regions. These different great regions are West Africa, East Africa, North Africa, South Africa, and Central Africa.
In West Africa, we have countries as Nigeria, Ghana, Togo, & Benin republic, etc.

In East Africa, we have countries as Uganda, Kenya, Tanzania, and others.
In North Africa, we have countries as Tunisia, Egypt, and others.
In Central Africa, we have countries as Cameroon, Central African Republic, Rwanda and others.
In South Africa, we have countries as South Africa, Namibia, Botswana, and others.

Great fine arts can be found in the beautiful countries of Africa. This defines the rich artistic endeavors of the Africa countries. It is observed that the African traditional outfits are very unique and colorful. The traditional garments were designed for the males and females. From my artistic observation, these traditional outfits are very rich and comfortable. The Custom styled African clothing can be found in the African countries. This is widly popular in the land of Africa. However, the African traditional outfits have widely spread to other countries of the world. This provides great opportunity for the people to benefit from the African traditional clothing.

# Examples Of One African Language: Yoruba

AFRICA

# EXAMPLES OF AFRICAN LANGUAGES

## TRANSLATION: DO WHATEVER YOU LIKE..

Creatively, languages can identify one's culture. Let us focus on the cultural aspect. Nigeria consists of ethnic groups and unique languages. There are great kingdoms, castles, kings (Oba), & queens within the cultural regions. There are great languages spoken in different ways. These great languages are Hausa, Yoruba, and Igbo. Creatively, I was able to speak the Yoruba language fluently and interpret it in words. These are examples of **Yoruba** language:

*Ba wo ni o se se?*
**Translation:** *How are you doing?*

*Aye o dun o*
**Translation:** *Life is sweet*

*O re mi*
**Translation:** *I am tired*

*O tu tu*
**Translation:***It is cold*

***Reference / info:***
***African movies***
Between Wilson and Broadway,
Chicago, IL(**north side**)

# Examples Of
# My Original Sketches
# Tribes

**Examples Of My Original Sketches**

# EXAMPLES OF MY SKETCHES: YORUBA

# SKETCHES OF YORUBA TRIBE

Sketching in abstract form

Since, I know about the artworks and languages of my culture. I will focus on what I have learned. Culturally, there are Hausa people, Yoruba people, and Igbo people. From my observation, Languages and great accents can be used to identify one's identity or culture. In this universe, **these three beautiful** languages can be observed within the unique cultural aspects. The world would be able to recognize the Africans by their great accents and cultural affairs. According to my observation, the facial expressions can be used to identify one's country (Cultural Background).

Previously, I visited one of the art museums in the United States. There were interesting historical art sculptures. Artistically, I was impressed that there were new advanced developments of arts. I found that the historical art exhibit of the Yoruba culture was available at periodical times. The art institute museum in Chicago consists of great artworks of the Yoruba culture. However, other works of arts were available. Check for art shows listing for updates.

# Facial Expressions:
# Animation

# EXPRESSIONS OF AFRICANS
## MY ANIMATION PROCESS

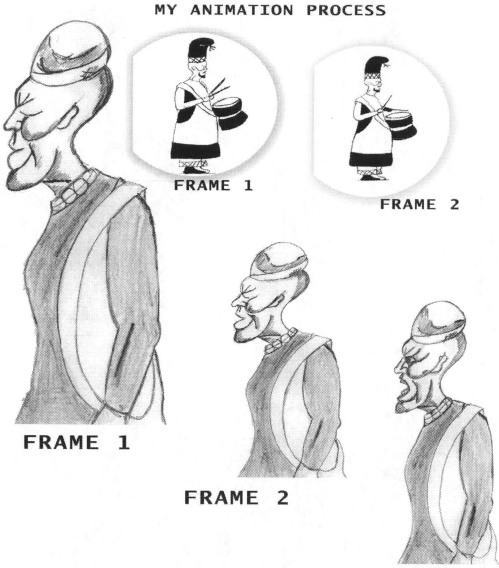

FRAME 1

FRAME 2

FRAME 1

FRAME 2

FRAME 4

FRAME 3 SKIPPED

*Sketches taken from motion capture picture – DAmo movies08*

# EXAMPLES OF MY SKETCHES

In this universe, we have natural facial expressions. These facial expressions are crying, smiling, happy, sad, and anxious, etc. In the movie industry, our facial expressions can be observed. In the real life scene, the computer animators are able to apply to what they see. The animators have to feel how real life actions are towards what they are producing. The animation sequence must be right and must blend well. The animation process is done in a frame by frame sequence. The animation speed ratio could be 10, 15, or 30 frames per second. Being an animator, I always use my tribal characters in my animation movies. Because I feel much comfortable, using what I have experienced in my culture. Most of my animation movies are engaged in the samples of my sketches. My characters have strong facial expressions. We can observe the facial expressions in this book. My life experience as a childhood can be observed on the faces of my characters.

# Africa And Other Heritages

# AFRICAN HERITAGE

**SKETCH**
OF AN AFRICAN GIRL

**SKETCH**
OF AN AFRICAN GIRL

In this universe, the artistic aspect and cultural aspect can be used to identify one's heritage. We have other great artworks from other great heritages. These other great heritages are African-American heritage, American heritage, Asian heritage, and others of the world. In this universe, we can see each country celebrating its heritage.

According to my culture, ceremony parties commence at evenings and ends through the following early morning (varies). The great Africans dress in their unique traditional outfits with colorful tops, colorful trousers, colorful skirts, & head gears (head ties). The women celebrate in head ties (called geles) and the men celebrate in their long robes (agbadas).

# Special Occasions Of Africa

# OCCASIONS OF AFRICA

## THE DANCING COUPLES

IMAGINATION By
Drawing Danola Taiwo

DSTAFRICA

Every country in Africa has its own great way of celebration. According to my culture, special occasions are celebrated in different ways. The wedding, birthday, and graduating ceremony can be performed in the church or a rented hall. According to my artistic cultural view and experience, some weddings are performed in the church (modernized). But not all are performed in the church (Depending on the religion).The African bridegroom wears suit and dressed shoes. The bride wears her wedding gown. The engagements of the lovely couples are performed in a traditional way. Decorated art ornaments can be observed on the traditional outfits. Creatively, the last celebration is performed in a party hall with a musician and drummers on the stage.

According to my cultural aspect of observation, the engagement ceremony is celebrated in a more defined traditional way (Yoruba). In a large hall, the engagement party is celebrated with crowds dancing, giving gifts, eating, drinking, and rejoicing. The African couples dance at the engagement party in their native wears. The invited guests rejoice and congratulate the lovely couples on their successful engagements. Later, the African couples are left in their lovely privacies. In a great way, we all celebrate our heritages and ceremony parties too. From my cultural view, I will always honor and cherish every heritage in the world (beautiful heritages).

# The African Dishes

Most of the African dishes are prepared in different sections. African food products are 100% natural and tend to have a very rich taste in flavors. As a reference to my experience, I have tasted large varieties of African dishes. Nigeria has a variety of dishes. The dishes are curry rice, jollof rice (red), fried rice, coconut rice, iyan, eba (Cassava), amala {Dried grinded yam}, and fufu. Some of the Nigerian dishes are spicy and seasoned. The Nigerian soups and stews come in different natural flavors. The Nigerian tasty and aromatic stews are obe egusi, okra soup, ewedu, efon, and ogbono soup. According to the African dishes, not every country has the same dishes. The African dishes taste different and definitely rich in flavors. According to my definition, I called it the great art of cooking.

***Great Restaurants / Great foods Info:***
African Restaurants: *Chicago, IL*
**Nigeria**
*Vee Vees African Restaurant*
*6232 N Broadway St, Chicago, IL*

*Nigerian kitchen*
*1363 W. Wilson Avenue. Chicago, IL*

*Bolat African cuisine Inc.*
*3346 N Clark St, Chicago & 4623 N Broadway St, Chicago, IL*

**Ethiopia**
*Ethiopia diamond restaurant*
*B/w Broadway /Thorndale **(North side}** Chicago, IL*

**Morocco: Moroccan**
*B/w Clark/Addison **(North side}**Chicago, IL*

*Damola Taiwo*

**Daata Darbar**
*2306 W. Devon Avenue Chicago, IL*

*Toham African restaurant*
*1422 W. Devon Avenue Chicago, IL*

**African food store: imports**
***World market b/w Broadway*** */ bryn mar, magnolia: Chicago, IL* **(north side)**
**Note: changes vary**

# Biography

Art is one of the strongest forces in the world. It can take anyone anywhere they wish to go. Art has an irresistible effect on most artists: especially the talented ones who do not know why they have been given these creative skills. Art is not something that can be given up easily. I have tried in the past to relinquish my dreams to become an artist, but I could not. My pencil would not leave me alone. When I have a pencil in my pocket; I can not resist the urge to draw. In fact, I will spend the entire day creating from my heart and soul.

The works I am exhibiting celebrates my life in Nigeria. Having been here in the states for the past 16 years. I always maintain my connection with my home. The colors, subject matter, and concepts stem from my everyday experiences in the place I call home.

# THE LONELY AFRICAN LADY
## DIRECTED BY
## DAMOLA TAIWO

DAMOLA AFRICAN STORYBOARD COPYRIGHT RESERVED 2008. 2 OF 1